FERNSEHTURM BERLIN

Stu Watson is a writer and artist who lives in Brooklyn, New York. A founder and editor of the literary journal *Prelude*, he teaches at Fordham University.

PRAISE FOR *FERSEHTURM BERLIN*

In *Fersehturm Berlin*, Stu Watson, mediumistically summons the formal ghost of Stéphane Mallarmé, with throws of a loaded 20-sided die. Words and phrases dance across the page, pop into huge, percussive font sizes, shrink tiny and intense, are channeled into regular prose forms. With a flair for irony (Ashbery and Morrissey are sampled here, among ancestors), Watson suspends disbelief in the face of historical catastrophes and wonders (Apollo 11's footprints on the moon, the Shroud of Turin, Princess Diana's obliteration)—and the rabbit holes and popular myths they engender. This is multifaceted, copious poetry blending succinct narration of world history with autobiographical tales and ruminations render poignant Watson's wide-ranging citations of before-time nuggets: skepticism lives in people born / long after these events occurred. Watson's gift is a clear, generous, humorous gaze. Here is courage for past, present, and future encounters, legends, wonders, heartaches. Listen and learn.
— Chris Hosea

With Mallarméan playfulness and intensity, Stu Watson turns the page into an interface in his latest book of poetry. *Fersehturm Berlin* interrogates casualties of Cold War geopolitical programs, royal conspiracies, the expectations of the past, and unrealized intimacies, becoming, like its title, both latent transmission and material testament of underdevelopment. "Impossible to shake the memory / of how we felt about what might yet be," Watson writes. With telescopic erudition and disarming vulnerability, he exhumes buried truths both private and public in this new vision or version of a speculative poetics.
— Chris Campanioni

Nothing's back, baby — yes, the anxious vacuity of Seinfeld and yes the zeros haunting binary code, but most of all the absence that is full of all that surrounds it, the impossible compulsory emptiness out of which, Stu Watson reminds us, each consciousness bursts forth. Martin Luther's, Sting's, even — maybe — that of the fourth-tallest free-standing structure in Europe. But how much of the chrysalis remains? Across his second collection, with open heart and ferocious mind, Watson recovers much of the nothing that we have done, and which we inherited from the violent nothings of horrible, humiliating twentieth century: 'battering our way through above / the old dead doldrums that here rule'.
— David B. Hobbs

Also by Stu Watson

Communicatingroups   (Mastadon Publishing, 2020)

ISBN: 978-1-916938-13-7

The author has asserted their right to be identified as the author of this Work in accordance with the Copyright, Designs and Patents Act 1988

Cover designed by Aaron Kent & Joseph Kent

Edited and Typeset by Aaron Kent

Broken Sleep Books Ltd
Rhydwen
Talgarreg
Ceredigion
SA44 4HB

Broken Sleep Books Ltd
Fair View
St Georges Road
Cornwall
PL26 7YH

Fernsehturm Berlin

Stu Watson

Broken Sleep Books

so much to learn
about the
Soviet space program

but still:
where did it lead?
to nothing-

ness the likes
of which
we'd only dreamed

before and
yet: here we are
reading in

our library bored
out of our
minds: body lulled

by this ripe summer
mood swelled
up to wash us down

in early 1955 the legal
status of space
still hadn't been defined

so would the Soviets
accept a flyover
by an American satellite?

their not protesting it
would help
establish the precedent

of course they claimed
that all of
this was for peaceful

purposes although
finally it
didn't matter

because Sputnik
beat the Americans
into space

along the western coast
of Ireland
Canadian bodies wash

ashore
are buried nearby
their plane

destroyed by u-boat
fire the
only monuments

to these
men are graves
they rest

all but forgotten
each one of 40
thousand Canadians

who gave their
lives as
part of a moral

obligation
or for other reasons
colonial

Egypt

there is a specter haunting

a scepter causing havoc
to bivouac
when faced with
torpedo attack

gripped

like my hand
cinching tight

the shopping sack

as I walk

from the store

through

the night

Napoleon is but a shallow
ghost a tomb
can hold
whereas with
Alexander there's no
question
of his even
being
buriable
too large to be anything
but printed
incised
burned
into metal

scored

when you're on the front line
you meet the enemy face to face
and he meets you

fast moving armored forces
impossible to avert at least at first
dinner of choices
  larder full of a passion for duck
     speed always a decisive factor in the early

days of war
   no one wants a part but when you have it then you come to need it
    like a segment in love with a sudden *triangularity*
     you welcome this new arrangement
      where you are instrument
       bled *blunt*

devastating fall of fire from the *sky*
  rain of bombs and bullets falling *planes*
   explosions everywhere
    children blown apart
     and there he is still grinning
      unloading *triggerfulls* in a dance
      parading like a miraculous error
      this haughty knowing order

        I remember being lost *there*

        on my first arrival
confused by how I was
supposed to orient myself and
find my way to where I would
be staying completely unable
to conjure a word in any
language overwhelmed staring
at the *tv needle* there

come as he kneels and prays
oh what will happen to us all
as crossing railway bells ring out
when all we know of how it goes
spread out on the dim whole steam unknown tracks rip word shaped holes

> right in an arm
> *and we shoot back as we are not*
> unable to *respond* and they
> *that minute seem to reverse field*
> and then they drove over the bones
> *as later we would*
> *also*

and they had wives and families but *that's a war*
and every Rommel launches his counterattack at once
and we cannot sustain our spirit in the rout
so long expected and likewise delayed
all things delayed under our grim regime
our mirthful sentimental rule

> of cards
>
> and uncut **thumbs**

completer sentences in the field

refer back **harder**

than the ***trim determiner*** allows
we'll all oscillate

it shows

after the crash/he brandished goods
reliant on ***draw***
too many empty
we *elongated* ones remain

zero blide
(*krigsmaskine*)

now **one** is being
nothingness **zero**
nothingness now one
of zero and **being**

the catapult is **full**
then **empty**
then **full**

etc

walls crumble before walled
ones zero in here

nothing to do
nothing to say

nothing to be

                              no matter what you are
                        there *he* is
                        where you should
                        be all but less
                        than HE whom

thunder

thunder

thunder

              let (it) be

made greater

like a sun

malady us Luther our old friend:

        resilient one take shape

        in cycles of nations even gods have fallen

off

        before Aztec: Toltec

        noble seeds

        beget a house

Behold: a new sun is risen

from clouds a new sun is born

quiz flipped

reorients itself

spectate the crowd watching

watch always for intensity of watching

and nothing else locked *a priori*

crowdsofpeoplealwayswalkingslowlyoverthebridge

a d j u s t i n g t o t h e n e w r e a l { i } t y

freshly experiencing

customs

relying on the dead

holding
hands
as if
across
a fissure
holding it
together

believing in those dead we knew
feeling obliged
we listen but do nothing rash at first because of course

ample doubts

persist (echo echo echo echo echo)

you make cloying remarks
a wall of Reuters reporters approaches

was it not wrong

turn the pages

slowly leave

the book's become too narrow
it's not your fault
it's the times
the times used
to be more
amenable
time used to be free

most days we sit at home nights
like waiting on a weekend that's
just the same finally no hope of
battering our way through above
the old dead doldrums that here rule

we all make mistakes

but some of us

pay double   triple

what   it   cost

us   to   return

blue faced from screaming

again it's that
much longer
if you allow for
the wait

grown gills from screaming

the power comes
in saying yes
like some
obsessive yes

eyes rising out on cones from screaming

<Sting plays obtrusively in the taxi>

the engine should be about caught up now
just get started on the   register receipts
somehow we've   got all of it to   keep track of
we need to keep   them at bay
        distracted, even

                                            too many days
                                            too little reliability
                                            in shade the
                                            delayed heat only
                                            delayed readability
                                            coming in a little later
                                            the same feeling but developed

Do you (you)
feel like I do?

know who it is when even
a stranger makes the door frame
rattle a little

the strangeness of staying in a stranger's home and feeling not quite like
a guest feeling uninvited feeling trapped by the circumstance but not
unwelcome forced into the situation by circumstances out of your control
contorted by circumstances into this situation out of your control and letting
go and even in doing that not learning but being silent showering wrong
somehow angering her by your showering the lack of a standing shower a
confusion a disaster of water everywhere oh so much water crossing over
the lip of the tub and then that long walk down into the center of the city
where the awful classes met the dreadful class unfolded boringly each day
every day and all I wanted to do was go out alone and wander and meet no
one and explore and think about the person I was then missing who seems
to me now almost as if he wasn't even real though of course he is it is they
are it was so I

j u m p r i g h t i n

i s t h e w a t e r w a r m e n o u g h

o n e w o n d e r s i f o n e i s b e i n g t o l d t h e w h o l e t r u t h

Princess Diana died
quite literally
of a broken heart

well she was a loose cannon
so many contradictory things

22

Diana had become so powerful
she was an enormous **threat**
an enormous **threat**
an enormous enormous enormous
threat
she had become a **threat**
she was a **threat** to their agenda
an enormous **threat** to their agenda
threatening their agenda enormously she
had to be removed and with her removal this
threat of course went away completely there
was no longer any **threat** at all the agenda has
since moved forward land mines everywhere
mines quite literally everywhere enormous
land mines everywhere now and the
fatal **threat** removed

you cannot trust old friends
they too much love your parents

it was on my penultimate night there that I met
him and even though nothing happened the
night has always stayed with me as an example
of what *might have* happened had I been
different more open not so terribly ashamed of
everything that had only so recently transpired
the insanity of living in a world like that of
trying to find your way through a nest of
realizing what was really happening not yet
imbued with newer purpose in connection
born not yet the purpose driven creature set
on course instead living as if under curse and
walking to the private garage where he kept
his *Lotus* I should have known and did know
and I let nothing happen and didn't go the next
day too hungover didn't meet him at the bar on
Gleimstraße near the *Mauerpark* where I lived
that summer where earlier I met the television
actors playing basketball and again think still of
all the things that didn't happen that wouldn't
happen the actions I couldn't take the obvious
actions because of who I was because of all of
my enormous obligations to myself and those
around me the imagined burdens I was then
still in the process of creating only of course
to have to decreate them later to decreate in
order to live just as to not sleep with someone
is sometimes the only possible way to

walk out of prison and right into the
Weimar Republic
wirklich gut
wirklich wirklich gut
und sollen wir die Bücher lesen
when under darkness lying lashed
when we are lashed here under darkness
lying
at last alone too dark to read and lashed
by an endless
dismay at who we still have not eclipsed inside of us that part

marginally better in the
breach   than in
sustaining   than in
its coils

                        than we
feel gripped
                    still   in
its coils
we can't compete with
perjury try as we might we
can't compete with those
who are better at bettering
themselves who take all
this so seriously and feel
no shame who reach for
what is workable and feel
no shame how we envy the
shamelessness as we dread
it in our shame

why trust in anyone?
why cavort with ghosts when
we have theater to believe in?

one doesn't think so much of suicide
when in Berlin

                                        but of course
                                        it has happened

Americans had wearied of men walking on the moon
we all felt good about it   we were pleased   we'd done   our job
the Soviets would never reach the moon   and that   as well
that pleases us   it gives us pride   we feel a surge of pride
our nation is   **triumphant**   but what next   no way to get
attention with the war already won   the cold war won

the shuttle program an   unmitigated error   bad
it cost much more than all the estimates   it was unsafe
more people died   (**fourteen**)   aboard the shuttle than in all
the other programs put together   plus the larger plan
originally called for space stations   these were not built
space stations orbiting the earth and moon   abandoned moon

the military interest in the moon remains strong
an ideal base for launching an attack impossible to
repel   though satellites might work as well   the moon perhaps
impractical   unless the Russians or the Chinese or
the French or Greeks should start on bases of their own   up there
why then we'd have no choice   we'd have to act   we'd get   to work

(thus 'science' is still subject to the vicissitudes of national rivalries; one of many problems)

if the moon landing was staged
it was the most elaborate play
within a play the world has ever
seen except unlike a play it was
universally believed as it unfolded
the skepticism lives in people born
long after these events occurred
long after the film stock had passed
into nostalgia long after our technology
had made all earlier technological eras seem
impossibly primitive by comparison

and if it was faked, what *were* those scientists all doing?

how do cell phones work?
is satellite tv a lie?
my GPS?

was Neil Armstrong *merely* the

world's

greatest crisis actor

and

nothing more?

he was more
much more
an Eisenhowerian
presence in American
life long after his heroically journeying to the moon

        humble and eschewing fame
        his model was **George
        Washington**

whose model was **Cincinnatus**
who may or may not have lived
(the records from that period
having been destroyed by Gauls)

        Armstrong retreated into capitalism
        he faded into money even as
        he tried to warn us what was
        happening to him along with everyone

but it was much

    much much much

        much much

          too late

the country's
        origins
           having sealed

               its
                fate

what's that?
a rat?
thank god

some other thing's survived the blast

still life enough in it
for me to

seize on

tear through Maya's veil
draw into paradox

learn nothing

eat

die

begin again in England
still the dream
begin again in England
become a different kind of **royal**

all troops were ordered to put on high density goggles to avoid retinal burns

green clusters fired as the final warning
tiny little mushroom cloud
heat blast and nuclear radiation

the battalion commander
would have had to implement a contingency plan

he   estimated   the   cost   of   revenge   in   this   case   to   be
too small to avoid

meet one's match in England
if it's not too late
if they've not driven her
to suicide

one thinks of suicide in England
always and with   mixed feelings

but was it even suicide?
no no no

13th pillar
65 miles per hour
tunnel by the river

and who are you?
if you kidnap me
you might find out
but you also might not

The Love Parade was an annual outdoor techno
music festival held in the *Tiergarten*. I attended
it with a number of my classmates, and we were
all much too buttoned up, even in our shorts
and t-shirts, for *The Love Parade*, which was
an affair that tended towards nudity. I can still
remember jello streaked bodies, red jello all
over the street like blood and music thrumming
as we walked and I was totally sober at least at
first, for the most part sober until perhaps later
in the day, but during the parade I was entirely
alert and shockingly present and the chaos all
around me looking back doesn't feel chaotic
outside of the woman covered in jello and the
shock on the face of my Chinese and Japanese
and Taiwanese and Korean and English friends
the other students from my introductory class
with whom I'd come to *The Love Parade*. I also
remember standing with them in the bar later
and reciting a poem about the *Owl of Minerva*,
an emblem of philosophy that Hegel tells us
'only spreads its wings at dusk' implying that
philosophy is always in and of itself belated;
that it arrives late, if at all; that it is reactive and
not proactive; that philosophy should stay out
of direct involvement in politics that politics is
best left to actors

please sing old owl
from the edge of sleep

out of the closet
endlessly rocking

>   things
>   registered by the mother need not
>   descend upon the son the dna allows for
>   differentiation in the traits by means of
>   an elaborate process that shuttles forth
>   recessive qualities without which we
>   would be transparently blended copies
>   more easily destroyed by disease   by life

men race seeking the body

I see your graying wings

your hooting cry

my eyes break

oh now we're going much too fast
we've already been captured
so many times before
why rush away
this time?

the son won't be happy about this
coincidence he's gone away to France?

some years after we'd visited it *The Love Parade* was shut
down because of an abundance of deaths among event
attendees. There are not too many other things that I
remember from my months living in Berlin. For the most
part I think I was thinking a lot about music and reading
all of the best novels of Thomas Hardy, that is, those
generally agreed to be the best, no second-rate Hardy
reader was I that summer in Berlin, looking out nightly at
the phone booth to which I'd walk to make my long calls
home to friends whichever ones I could get on the line,
long landline conversations then still common then still
possible the only way of keeping in close touch besides
email which as now was easily ignorable more ignorable
than a call I found at any rate

arrange a meeting with the boy
we'll set all things in order for
the funeral

it seems to me you lived it seems to me you lived your life it seems to me your life lived itself like life living itself you seemed to me to live your life like a candle the candle seemed to be like your life it seemed to me living my life it seemed to my life you lived your life like a candle in the wings waiting in the wings even after you'd taken the stage somehow it seemed like that living my life like a candle on top of a mountain somehow still alight despite the infernal wind which you seem to have lived your life like to me seemed to me only to me always to me it is me this is really about this seeming what it seems is what it is candle in the wind it is only so much apparitional appearing like wind itself completely transparent and yet still tangible that is how the theater seems to me

kill the medium
not the messenger

media are our
hours' enemies
a nemesis
decrying us

the Vikings did not invent piracy
although they may have brought
it to its European zenith
from the Caspian
to Newfoundland
their long ships
partaking in deadly work

did anyone happen to catch
the color of the flag they flew?
such operations in the North
Sea once would have been all
but unthinkable but here we
are new ravagers emerging
again from out of Norway
disrupting our diplomancy

and this is where we must fill up
there's no choice and we have to stop
I don't fear everybody looking
but they will and are and will
continue because they don't know
and I've not time enough or
energy to explain I just want
to get my gas and be on my way
I've got a funeral to attend too many
things have been rearranged in our lives
lately I've been changing and it's
not something I'm really prepared for
the questioning the looks the people wanting
to know *are they real* the eyes raised
the frightened looks of children *how*
can they be real? they seem to be saying
even as they are staring silently right at them
staring right above my eyes
staring right at the nodules
the pointed nubs now poking
out on my brow still making
just little tents there of my skin
just starting to emerge as now
the transformation has finally begun
and I am to become fully what I am
almost but for the final splitting
and the call I'll feel the noise the voice
inside of me whose throat I'll open
the voice whose blood I'll spill out on the sidewalk
when I can finally at last begin to speak

Geraldo's in makeup
he's thinking it over

the President warned me
we'd lose it on cue

is there any point in asking for
forgiveness for a deed that you
don't even begin to regret?

what does it really
mean to be guilty of
a crime of which you
are not yet aware?

would a limousine seat belt law
have made all the difference?

psychosomatic?

addict?

insane?

I was with her when she died

England rose to the occasion

the hospital sheet impressed
with her dying image
in a nuclear reaction?
too much to hope for?
even just a plain old x-ray?

Alexander had a tomb once but
talked most of his mother

more than 60 priests died
merely thinking about it brings death
Italian society faced real jeopardy

keep the shroud behind glass
it isn't ready to be seen
it's very shy

he sought not his father's killers
over long
                    for it was said were
he to have looked too hard he
would invariably have found
himself to be among the guilty

the radiocarbon dating of the
shroud places it firmly in the
medieval period yet despite
these verifiable results a number
of believers have insisted that
the portion of the cloth snipped
off for testing in the 1970s was
actually an *obvious* medieval patch
interpolated into the shroud to
repair damage from a fire the fire
having perhaps itself further added
to the contamination of the data

as lucrative as a successful bank-raid, man,
the Romans are to blame for so much shit,
but Alexander was more savage than
the Caesars any way you reckon it

        as bedposts have gone lately out of style,
        as marmalade retreats into the past,
        so our watched pots with haste begin to boil,
        all our blood covered leaves fall now so fast

claymation realer than the twisted edge
that photoshop distortion lends to life
the team not great, not good, but average,
a sailor suit has never worn a wife

        magnetic pull out there beyond the moon
        the reading and rereading of the tides
        the tragically aware pulled down too soon
        to where the lonesome adversary hides

blocked off above the seething sheets of ice | a dromedary camel marches on
| we sling the stones right at the cockatrice | ignoring us she parlays into dawn
| dead heartbeat for the listening stethoscope | and we will not come after,
not by long | bitumen spitting hydrant ringed with smoke | the screaming
silenced by the stricken gong | come out the air raid's over, siren's dead | the
blisters on our arms begin to rise | our one friend has been wounded in the
head | the other lost her legs below the thighs | no palliative care is possible
| no remedy exists to solve this wound | we stare into the silence of the full |
moon searing us

into the ground

our image on the wall is but the shadow of right action | the hermit strikes when you have turned your back | the malcontent distills his pain and worships every bottle he forces the waiting idle world to drink | so many ways to ring the earth with poison | contamination everybody's game | more static than the eagles pressed on coins | demonstrative as a reluctant king | priced just to sell to get rid of the stock | abortive fantasy about the market | the pressure of the failure reaching in and taking up more space incessantly in your daily life until you realize there is no way out except through further battening down of hatches already tightened well past bursting so to bursting then we go | the shadows of old friendships corrupting your memories of family | a disease that shook the whole house silently like a tremor | the riddles the sphinx didn't have the chance to use | the riddle she did and all the bodies that it claimed | the gender of the sphinx transforms somewhere between Egypt and Greece as does its shape its form | you can't live up to people's inflated and frankly stupid ideas about the past | idolized periods were all unbearably awful | the American people know almost no one whose life has been affected by the reality of shrapnel | the depleted uranium used as recently as the 1990s in shell casings is of little concern to anyone anywhere in the entire world | most of Rome's greatest heroes conveniently die at the height of their fame | of those who do not almost none are revered except for Augustus | but of course this is all speculative as what we know about any of these people was filtered entirely through the propaganda machinery of the day | this machinery existed even if you don't believe it did | there are many things like that that persist even in the face of your personal disbelief | this experience is called cognitive dissonance | cognitive dissonance and our ability to experience it and yet still function relatively coherently is among humanity's greatest strengths | without cognitive dissonance there would be no death penalty | in the land of icicles the bicycle is king | an isosceles triangle will always offend me | people need to be responsible about misleading the young people | the future leaders of our world | one in five Americans today will admit to harboring doubts | the way the expressions of confidence persist in a society gone bankrupt | it is in the nature of things impossible to tell the precise moment when things turn | when dies the king or falls the president | his promises ignored or become law | when either way not because they are easy but because they are heard | the rocket faked | the elevator delivering them to the command module | also taking them right back down | the line of descent from father to son generally uninterrupted | how else allow a usurpation except that the prince is absent? | how can the flames be flickering when there is no moon out on the parapet | the balustrade you stand at there above the moat | where I've so long kept watch | and you're sure it was his voice? | it can't be stressed enough the cause of death was driver recklessness and that alone | apparent primitiveness breeds arrogance | sincerity breeds conservatism | they act like no one died in the run up to Apollo when of course three people did | what happened to the Irish monks the Vikings found in Iceland remains a mystery | their currach boats could not have breached | the Denmark Strait? We do not know | they may have been intercepted on their way | washed up in England | as Viking boats once floated down the Seine | there by the tunnel connecting the river roadway to the city center | bearded Vikings disembarked on that little island at the heart of Paris | and took what they could before darting away | these lightning tactics a recurring theme across time | Arab horsemen of the period using parallel maneuvers on land | the idea of being stationary itself a threat | until the rise of castles | but with them rose towers of moisture | enormities of dampness gather for the first time here | breeding ground for spirits of decay | humidities perplexing all demanding some relief | some stay for flies and mosses that will hang | if something isn't done | the tapestries are mouldering even as the King holds court | in many cases the shadows on the moon are not parallel | not even Napoleon finally knew what to do | if something's visible you already know it is reflecting light | in a windless environment | which knows what to say next:

THE FLAG SWINGS LIKE A SHEET OF CHAINMAIL WOULD

TRY IT AT HOME SEE FOR YOURSELF IT'S TRUE

dark now sitting here
alone formulaically
broken in half on being
deserted skeptic half rid
myself of him clicked
closed the shutters saw
ivy vines begin to clutch
and ripped them off
striving to right
myself   clarity cut
down on all the crap
and so we're all alone
again it's like we never
left

                                        please me off yeah
                                        ascending curtain flaw
                                        spiraling thread tear
                                        running against
                                        gravity gaining ground
                                        updrifting entropy
                                        stake me for yes
                                        I watch mind make
                                        it collapse and cling
                                        here leaning on the balcony
                                        jutting out here leaning
                                        looking out on neighbors
                                        quarreling together loudly

they say the radiation
falling down kills all
feeling as it strips away peels
your paint but that's
not right it's painful very painful
also like a fighting it you'd try what mourns you

it's weird there's all of this for such a tiny plot
of land it's like we haven't thought
about it at all we want what we can't have
implicitly no doubt about that now pave
over the old underground bunker where
we once danced weekly for
our pay so discreetly no one knew
it was even us the figured masks peeled off in due
course and you grew tired of it and I longed to leave
Berlin and find a country where to grieve
was not to lie all still so caught up here
in the reforming we are getting under
way still working hard to change ideas
fix all the scaffolding of what once was
our city now our ruin now our doom
the necklace we have slung off like the spume
of smoke there rising from the crater
that place that used to be our theater
smoke careening up and breaking out
departing yes that's what it's all about

       hold back a minute more
       I see a glove upon the shore
       beside the old river lapped
       still through the smell of gasoline trapped
       skeletons some guilty and some innocent
       the bodies mixed into the new foundation bent
       metal rods stuck into wet cement
       the Reichstag now a Parliament
       look there goes Willy Brandt
       he's smiling like a revenant

              perhaps when the election
              falls on him when he has won
              I'll finally see a way
              that I can get back in and stay

              from pouring hopes into political
              reforms I fear that we've grown cynical

be all sins recovered in the climate of denial | exhume for yourself the buried truths pretending they're too difficult to claim | decorate fluently the snow capped television set | rent out the college rent it for the movies | disband the college use its buildings just for movies | keep the money moving finally that's the motivation | assume the movies will take care of the college | despise yourself if you are proven wrong | too harshly so you then compound the problem | reflecting on the long chain of decisions | that led to this, the wasting of your life | come back I'm not yet finished my haranguing | there are these spots of mustard on the couch | it's like they've been burned in somehow | though really they just dripped on there last night | oh him? don't be concerned, it's not contagious | a scientist's experiment gone wrong | or just slightly awry | the lizard glands implanted did not take | the course that we expected when he first | decided to submit to the procedure | it's really just a melancholy mood | impossible to shake the memory | of how we felt about what might yet be | but now it's now and, well, the chainsaws are late in starting | three more blocks to be constructed just this week | yep the whole forest will soon just be a memory | they're dynamiting stumps to lay foundations | they're even gonna drain the lake | fill it up with concrete | make it into a natural skatepark | the plans these zany kids enact when they have money | compromise on Florida, why bother? | I saw a sick one crucify an elf | though maybe it was just a doll | the elves all died off | broke all elf necks myself in fact | but still it's not right crucifying anything | not when you've just cut down a forest to build sudden enormous condos | there's no need for sacrilege when ignoring something is more powerful | don't bother to do anything | withhold and you have won | a paradox but one that gives you power | all paradoxes love to give you power | it helps them see their value | in this topsy-turvy world

that summer was one of many periods
in which I was so consumed by absent things
by absent people and places that even
surrounded I was drawn into myself siphoned
and angry somehow at the silence
which I knew would fall away so casually
when we met again socially in the fall
though in a sense it never really recovered
from that rupture that was the time I
associate most with things moving apart
finally so I was in Berlin by myself for
more than two months and it was a
kind of apocalypse with all things rushing
and me taking insane weekend jaunts
to Florence or to Amsterdam the fares
so cheap the hotels so cheap my preferences
have never been for anything fancy
and during the week I'd sit blinded by
boredom in German language class apparently
absorbing more than I realized at the time
because I later passed a German reading exam
without much preparation though as I recall
I failed the one I took from the department
at Yale which had rather higher standards
in all probability than I did and I think I
still kept all my phone numbers in my
wallet or had just memorized them sitting in
that phone booth calling friends talking
for hours about all manner of things
I remember my friend's father answering
once and when I said I was in Florence
he asked "Florence, Massachusetts or
Florence, Italy?" And I said "The latter,"
having never heard of this later Florence
out there by Amherst just by 91 a place
I'd driven past hundreds of times already
then which now I haven't been by for years

what if Diana ordered him to do it?
in that case can she lay in consecrated ground?
she does, at any rate, out on an island
on her noble family's estate—it can't be found
by curious visitors, not easily, not without
the proper permission to pay a visit—
Elton John comes twice a year
just to be near
to her
again—

                              but it's
                    not true he never comes
                it's much too much for him still
                    even now these decades later
                        he likes to think however
                of the fish that swim in the pond
                    that spreads out all around her
                sheltered tomb he likes to think
                    of their roaming eyes down in
                the murk and lilypads fish eyes
                    live and angling for food

                                        'I order you to
                                        drive us into
                                        the 13th pillar
                                        of the tunnel
                                        with as much
                                        speed as you can
                                        conveniently
                                        accumulate.'
                                        'Oui, madame.'

here lies the water: go

when graves have op'd their sleepers we'll have peace

or when he sings again that old sad song

asked by her sons asked only by her sons to play the song he says he'll do it then

it's always the Norwegians who are the problem in the West

it's not the Danish nor the Swedes, never the Finns nor Russians, Germans, Mamalukes, nor Turks

and it will fall to him to bring to order what is left if anything at all is left if it's not all been run into the ground

a missile that's exploded in its silo can't be used
it won't be fired it instead stands
a warning beacon or a charred locus
for fear a blackened beacon for Fortinbras

                              Titan II
                              about you
                              there is now no more to do
                              you have been given over for solid fuel
the tunnel walls close in
               we've said
                         the things that made us begin

               to speak
                         and not those things we know

Always crashing in the same tunnel

the first Americans were coastally adapted

the seaboard was dotted

headland to headland

they killed

and moved

killed

moved

what is to be gained

in killing her like that

not much but people thinking

it might matter makes

a potentially useful distraction

unless in the Gulf of Mexico

they lost their way

drifted out to Cuba

caught up in the gulf stream

blown to Denmark once again

Columbus himself would deny it
the flatness of this world
he would deny it
like the king
he thought
he was
to be
so
soon
if everything
went according to
plan if all his actions
added up to what he thought
they would if all of it finally could
be pulled off without a hitch a usurpation
of an entire new and largely unspoilt continent

it isn't that I never learned to love Berlin
it's that it never came to feel sufficiently
like home it never held me like I wanted
it to hold me it wasn't right I wasn't
right it's been now twenty years I must
go back and face it what I was then who
I am now all I might be I must live up at
least a little to what I have inherited and
not just dawdle here at my own personal
Wittenberg forever when out there just
out there where I have been now that
the real thing waits

can't go in yet for fighting if you try | the relics are all hidden in the tower | the bodies of those killed along the way | much later they'll be set up on the stage | for everyone to see and to admire | as she had asked as he would want, you know | there's no hope of avoiding it, I fear | the regulations are always obeyed | and, yes, especially when the king is dead | the prince is dead the queen all dead they're dead | the princess too is dead though she had left | the prince of course some years ago it's not | much matter now it does not take up space | once they've been shown we'll all be off | we'll claw our way up where we started fine | a place where we can start again without | the need for castles or a monarchy | I just heard of a rumor from the North | they speak of distant lands that we now own | I'm not quite sure just where, consult the prince | when he returns he will have learned of much | his education now nearing its end | and just in time, the king, his father, dead | eyes covered with a pair of rich doubloons | flesh food for all the tunneling raccoons | that tower where the kingdom knew its joy | now wrestles to death the enigmatic specters | stabs right through the heart of the blind arras | intoxicated as a river gorged | and glutting me remorse I cannot stay | turned morbid fancy at the death of queens | and princesses done fast to death in France | Horatio, oh stay, my friend it knows | not what it does, this tale to me, me still | untrod upon in biding here my time | here as I wait enthralled and stunned as if | I had been poisoned 'mid the very act

Go, bid the silos shoot

Acknowledgments

Earlier versions of sections of this book appeared in *Denvery Quarterly* and *Powder Keg*.

Thank you to Aaron Kent for his editorial eye and for believing in this project.

Thank you to Robert C.L. Crawford, Chris Hosea, and Armando Jaramillo Garcia for reading previous iterations of this manuscript.

This work would not have been possible without my poetry teachers and mentors who have moved beyond: John Hollander, Brett Foster, and Craig Arnold.

Lastly, thank you to my parents and siblings for their support, and to my friends Lucy Greene, Sam Mickens, Evan Carmouche, Catherine Engh, George Weinberg, David Hobbs, and Josh Schneiderman for ongoing dialogue.

LAY OUT YOUR UNREST

www.ingramcontent.com/pod-product-compliance
Lightning Source LLC
LaVergne TN
LVHW041237080426
835508LV00011B/1249